Contents

War in art   2

The First World War   4

Asking everyone to help   6

Official war artists   8

Camouflage art   10

The artist-soldiers   12

Painting the wounded   14

Animals at war   16

War machines   18

Landscapes of war   20

The home front   22

Women at work   24

Peace and remembrance   26

Glossary   28

Index   29

The uses of war art   30

Written by Jillian Powell

War in art

Wars have been fought throughout history. The first images of war that we have were made by artists.

Greek and Roman coins often showed soldiers fighting or horses charging to war. Pictures of battles were carved on tombs and grand arches to celebrate victories. Artists were paid to show armies looking strong and powerful as they defeated their enemies.

This carving of a battle is nearly 2000 years old and is on the side of a Roman tomb.

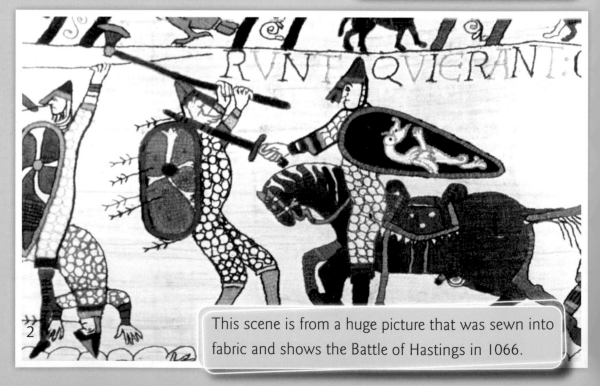

This scene is from a huge picture that was sewn into fabric and shows the Battle of Hastings in 1066.

2

In the 1400s, this artist used bright colours and real gold to make his picture of a battle look impressive. He was asked to paint it to celebrate the victory of the winning side.

3

The First World War

The First World War was fought between Britain and Germany and their **allies**. It lasted for four years from 1914 to 1918 and was fought on land, on sea and in the air. It killed around 16 million people.

When the war began in August 1914, the British government needed men to join the army and wanted support from the public. They used artists to create images for posters that would persuade men to fight for their country and their families to support them.

5

As the war went on, some of the poster artists created images to show people at home how they could help. The pictures reminded people that everyday things, like saving food or using less coal to heat their bathwater, supported the **war effort**.

The poster artists got their message across by linking everyday things to soldiers, ships and weapons.

DO **YOUR** BIT!

SAVE FOOD

F.C. 54.   HAZELL, WATSON & VINEY L? LITHO, LONDON

Official war artists

Soon after the war began, the British government sent two photographers to France and Belgium, where the enemy armies were fighting. Their job was to make images to **promote** the war at home.

Ernest Brooks was the first official photographer of the First World War. He took thousands of pictures.

Ernest Brooks in 1916

This is one of Brooks's photos. His photos are dramatic but were often posed to show soldiers' bravery.

The first **official war artist**, Muirhead Bone, was hired by the government in 1916. They chose him because they thought his drawings would look powerful when they were printed in magazines. He made hundreds of small drawings, mostly in black and white and full of realistic detail. Some were quick sketches made on the spot, showing troops in action or buildings damaged by war.

This sketch by Muirhead Bone is of Welsh soldiers.

Earlier artists often worked from stories and their imaginations. Unlike them, Bone and the artists who followed him saw what it was really like to fight a war.

Camouflage art

The government also paid artists to make maps or drawings to help British spies and to do **camouflage** painting to trick the enemy.

Leon Underwood made spy posts camouflaged as trees. He also made paintings like this one, recording the kind of work he did. The men are setting up a fake tree for a spy to hide inside and observe the enemy.

Some artists were paid to paint camouflage patterns called "dazzle" on ships to protect them at sea. Dazzle camouflage made it hard for enemy ships and **submarines** to tell the size of British ships and the direction they were going.

In this painting, the artist John Fergusson makes some shapes look **3D** and others look flat. His style uses strong colours and broad brush strokes.

This picture of a camouflaged ship confuses our eyes, just as the dazzle painting on real ships confused the enemy.

The artist-soldiers

Many artists joined the army to serve as soldiers. Eric Kennington was one of them.

Kennington was wounded in 1915 and sent home. In England, he completed a painting of himself with his friends resting after a battle during the war. It was shown at a gallery in London. For the first time people saw how hard it was for soldiers fighting in the war.

Unlike the poster artists, Kennington shows soldiers looking cold and tired.

ERIC H KENNINGTON

It became clear that the war was going to be long and brutal. In 1917, the British government asked more artists, including many already serving as soldiers, to record what they saw happening around them.

Like many soldiers, the artists saw men who had become good friends being injured and killed. Many artists felt a duty to show the full horror of the war.

In this drawing the artist shows us the effect that one soldier's death has on another.

SALVAGE.

13

Painting the wounded

John Singer Sargent was a famous portrait painter who was asked by the government to create a large **memorial** picture about the war. He chose to paint wounded soldiers.

Gas was used as a weapon for the first time in the First World War. It burnt the skin, lungs and eyes. Sargent's painting shows gas victims being led off the battlefield. It is a huge picture, and the figures in it are almost life-size.

The setting sun and pale colours help to create a sad mood. Some of the soldiers are dead and many have bandages where they are injured.

When the painting was put on display in 1919, people were very moved by it and it was voted "picture of the year".

Animals at war

Some artists painted the animals which had been sent to war. They included dogs, pigeons and around a million horses and **mules** that were used by the **cavalry** or to pull weapons, ambulances and supply wagons.

In the middle of this painting, the artist shows a line of mules, trapped by exploding **shells** as they try to cross the battlefield.

Edwin Noble was an army vet and war artist who painted many pictures of war horses. Some record the injuries they suffered. Others, like this painting, make us feel sorry for the animals that were involved in the war.

This horse is lost in No Man's Land, the wasteland between enemy trenches. It looks thin, sick and very alone.

War machines

When the war began, new inventions were changing the world. People were excited by the first cars and aeroplanes. Artists tried to show this excitement by painting the shapes and speed of the new machines.

The war speeded up the design and building of aeroplanes and tanks, and the war artists showed them in action.

Tanks were often shown as if they were great unstoppable beasts.

Small planes were used to map enemy trenches to help troops aim guns and shells directly at their targets. There were often midair gunfights between planes.

The British plane is being chased by several German planes. It looks as if they are diving towards us in a great cloud of smoke.

Landscapes of war

The battles of the First World War destroyed the countryside. Soldiers dug open tunnels called trenches. Shells left huge craters or holes in the ground and trees were blasted to stumps.

Landscape painters usually painted beautiful scenes. But the war artists had to find new ways to paint the battered landscapes that they saw. They took ideas from new styles of art that were appearing, like Cubism, and began to use hard outlines, simple shapes and dull colours.

This painting shows two soldiers trying to find their way along a road. The trees look like steel posts. Craters caused by explosions have filled with rain. Concrete blocks and bits of iron and barbed wire litter the ground. Nothing seems to be living.

Here, artist Paul Nash shows that war destroys everything it touches.

The home front

The war changed lives at home too. The government wanted to show how ordinary people lived and worked in wartime. They sent war artists, including women painters like Anna Airy, to visit factories to show workers making shells and other weapons. The workers were women, and men who were too old to fight. They are shown as busy and hard-working, all playing their part to help the war effort.

When Airy worked on this painting of a **forge** where shell cases were being made, it was so hot that her shoes were burnt off her feet.

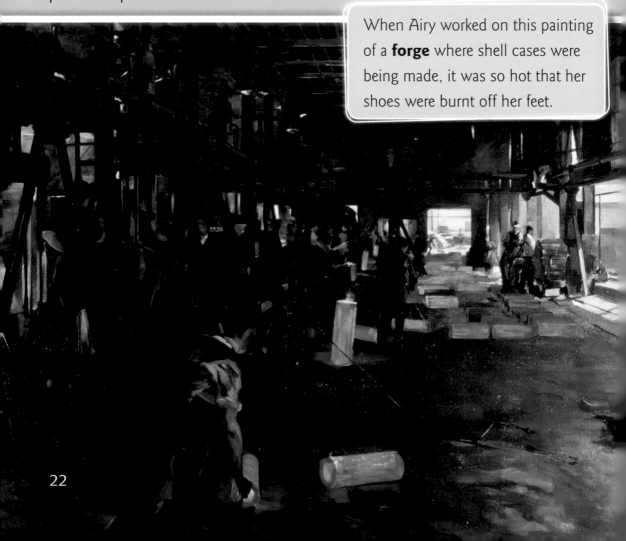

During the war, enemy ships and submarines stopped British ships from bringing in food, so shops ran short of many goods. **Rationing** was introduced to make sure that everyone got their fair share. People had to queue up to buy food.

In this picture by CRW Nevinson, the dark colours and sad faces of the women in a queue for food show that everyday life was becoming hard.

Women at work

Several painters were paid to paint women at work in wartime. They showed how women's lives were changing as they took over the jobs that used to be done by men.

This picture shows two women working with metal in an aircraft factory.

Other women joined the Women's Land Army, which trained them to work on farms and allotments. They were known as land girls.

These women are working on a farm alongside prisoners of war. Their uniforms remind us that they are also fighting for their country.

These sisters do different kinds of war work. One works on a farm, another is a nurse who cares for wounded soldiers and the third works in a weapons factory.

Peace and remembrance

When the war ended, war artists recorded the peace meetings and victory parades. But people no longer saw war as a glorious adventure. War artists had helped to show what many had seen and felt – how cruel and deadly war could be.

The war artists made around 3,500 images that still help to shape the way we see and think about the First World War.

This picture of a parade celebrating peace shows women who were nurses and ambulance drivers in the war.

Today, digital images can be sent back from **war zones** instantly. But we still need war artists to help us understand the feelings of soldiers and how war affects people and places.

soldiers training in Afghanistan

Here, the artist shows soldiers from many different countries to make us think of ways they are all the same.

27

Glossary

3D	a way of painting or drawing that makes images look deep and solid, like real objects
allies	countries which join together to fight
camouflage	patterns that help to disguise people or objects by making them blend in with their surroundings
cavalry	soldiers who fight on horseback
forge	a workshop where things are made out of metal
memorial	created to help people remember an event
mules	animals that are part donkey and part horse
official war artist	an artist paid by the government to record their experience of war in drawings and paintings
promote	to raise awareness and support
rationing	controlling the food supply by giving people coupons to buy only their fair share
shells	bombs made by filling steel cases with explosive materials
submarines	sea ships that can travel on or underwater
war effort	joining together to try and win the war
war zones	places where there is fighting between enemy armies

Index

Anna Airy   22

battlefield   14, 16

colours   3, 11, 15, 20, 23

CRW Nevinson   23

drawings   9, 10

Edwin Noble   17

Eric Kennington   12

Ernest Brooks   8

gas   14

horses   2, 16, 17

John Fergusson   11

John Singer Sargent   14

Leon Underwood   10

Muirhead Bone   9

mules   16

Paul Nash   21

photographers   8

posters   4, 12

rationing   23

shells   19, 20, 22

ships   6, 11, 23

sketches   9

spy posts   10

submarines   11, 23

trenches   17, 19, 20

war effort   6, 22

weapons   6, 16, 22, 25

women   22, 24, 25

wounded   12, 14, 25

The uses of war art

celebrating victories

YOUR COUNTRY'S CALL

Isn't this worth fighting for?
ENLIST NOW

encouraging people to join the army

showing what war is really like

promoting the war

DO **YOUR** BIT!

SAVE FOOD

supporting the war effort at home

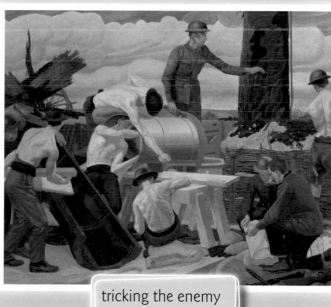
tricking the enemy

Ideas for reading

Written by Gillian Howell
Primary Literacy Consultant

Learning objectives: *(word reading objectives correspond with White band; all other objectives correspond with Diamond band)* continue to apply phonic knowledge and skills as the route to decode words until automatic decoding has become embedded and reading is fluent; identifying and discussing themes and conventions in and across a wide range of writing; summarising the main ideas drawn from more than one paragraph; retrieve, record and present information from non-fiction

Curriculum links: Art and Design, History

Interest words: camouflage, images, tomb, celebrate, allies, photographers, imaginations, brutal, pigeons, craters, Cubism, rationing, queue

Word count: 1,735

Resources: pens, paper, internet

Getting started

- Read the title and look at the cover illustration together. Ask the children to suggest what the illustration shows and say how the picture makes them feel.

- Discuss with the children the purpose of the book. Ask them what they expect to find out by reading this book. Turn to the back cover blurb to confirm their ideas.

- Ask the children to read the contents list. If children struggle with *camouflage*, ask them to break it into chunks and explain the pronunciation of the last syllable with a long vowel sound and soft *g*. Ask them to suggest other strategies they could use to work out new words, e.g. contextual clues from the pictures, phonics strategies.

Reading and responding

- Ask the children to read the text and, as they read, make notes of the purpose and uses for the different types of war art.

- Ask them to pause on p4 and find the word *allies*. Ask them to say why bold print is used for this word – that it is in the glossary. Ask them to find the glossary and read the definition of the word.